WHAT GOD SAYS ABOUT JESUS

I.D. Campbell

Copyright © 2012 I.D. Campbell

All rights reserved.

ISBN-13: 978-1484000915

ISBN-10: 1484000919

This Book is dedicated to Yahya Luqman Saleem.

CONTENTS

		pg
	Acknowledgments	
1	Introduction..	1
2	Zakariya (pbuh)...	4
3	John the Baptist (pbuh)..	7
4	Mary the Mother of Jesus (pbuh).................................	10
5	Young Jesus (pbuh)..	16
6	The Gospel according to Jesus'(pbuh)........................	21
7	The Holy Spirit...	24
8	Jesus (pbuh) the Miracle Worker.................................	27
9	Jesus (pbuh) the Messenger...	31
10	Jesus (pbuh) the Messiah..	34
11	Not Killed or Crucified..	37
12	The Corruption of Jesus' (pbuh) Message.................	40
13	Trinity...	46
14	Son of God?..	49
15	Jesus (pbuh) the Witness..	56
16	Hope...	59
17	Jesus' (pbuh) Successor..	61
18	No Distinction..	66

What God Says About Jesus

ACKNOWLEDGMENTS

First and foremost, Alhamdulillah. All praise is due to Allah. He is the source of all truth, therefore all that I convey of the truth in this book and in life are because of Allah, and only the mistakes are from me.

Introduction

There are three great monotheistic religions in the world today, Judaism, Christianity and Islam, and there is one person separating these three giants, JESUS (pbuh). To most Christians, he is the Lord and Savior of the world. He is God in the flesh, which came to this earth to show his love for mankind by taking on the sin of the world. To most Jews, he is a false Messiah and a false prophet. For the Muslim, Jesus (pbuh) falls in between these two extremes. To Muslims, he is neither God, nor a false prophet, but a mighty messenger and servant of God. Muslims believe that Jesus (pbuh) was the Messiah that the Jews have awaited and whom they still await.

Because of Jews' perception of Jesus (pbuh), they reject his teachings and they look for the "true" Messiah to come. Because of Christians' understanding of Jesus (pbuh), their every want and need is met through their belief in Jesus (pbuh). As God incarnate, he is the ultimate path to Heaven. The Muslim considers Jesus (pbuh) to be one prophet in the long line of prophets and because he was the final prophet to the Jewish people, Muslim maintain that another prophet was sent after him, who would be a prophet for the whole of mankind.

Jews make up about 13 million people in the world today. 1.8 billion people on earth are Muslims and 2.2 billion people are

Christian. Isn't it a shame that so many people's paths diverge from one point? There are 6.8 billion people on earth. If these three groups could get together and come to an agreement on this one issue, 4 in every 7 people on earth would share a common path and a common goal. I have written two books which address the nature, the message and the life of Jesus (pbuh) and I have written another book discussing the beliefs of those who adhere to the principles of Judaism taught in the Jewish Torah. These three books can help explain why Muslims, Jews and Christians believe as they do. These books also attempt to reconcile these three perspectives and formulate a conclusion and an answer to the question, Who Is Jesus?

Al-Qur'an 4:171
O People of the Scripture(Jews and Christians)! Do not exaggerate in your religion nor utter aught concerning Allah save the truth. The Messiah, Jesus son of Mary, was only a messenger of Allah

Jesus Christ (pbuh) lived 2000 years ago, yet he remains an extremely important figure to more than half of the people on the planet today. In the Muslim's holy book, Al-Qur'an, the man known to most of the world as Jesus Christ (pbuh) was a messenger of Islam, both respected and revered by 1.8 billion Muslims worldwide. Most of the world, who knows of Jesus (pbuh), gets their picture of him from the New Testament of the Bible. Many people are unaware of what the Qur'an has to say about this transcending figure of human history. The Qur'an is the words of God revealed to the man Muhammad (pbuh). This is my effort to express the Qur'anic and the Islamic understanding of one of the mightiest messengers and prophets of God, Isa ibn Mariam-Jesus son of Mary (pbuh). [In ancient Aramaic, his name is Eesho which sounds quite similar to the Arabic "Isa" pronounced Eesa.]

To avoid confusion, it should be explained from the onset that the Arabic language, like the Hebrew language, uses 2 kinds of plurals. One plural is the plural describing a number greater than 1 and the other plural is a plural of respect for majesty and sovereignty. The Qur'an uses the plural of respect oftentimes when describing God, because he is the most deserving of this honor. Therefore when one reads "We" and "Us" in the Qur'an, they should not confuse it with a belief in more than one God.

Zakariya (pbuh)

We begin the story of Jesus (pbuh) with the tale of another prophet of God, Zakariya (pbuh).

> ### *Al-Qur'an 3:38*
> **There did Zakariya pray to his Lord, saying: "O my Lord! Grant unto me from Thee a progeny that is pure: for Thou art He that heareth prayer!**
> ### *Al-Qur'an 3:39*
> **While he was standing in prayer in the chamber, the angels called unto him: "Allah doth give thee glad tidings of Yahya, witnessing the truth of a Word from Allah, and (be besides) noble, chaste, and a prophet,- of the (goodly) company of the righteous."**
> ### *Al-Qur'an 3:40*
> **He said: "O my Lord! How shall I have son, seeing I am very old, and my wife is barren?" "Thus," was the answer, "Doth Allah accomplish what He willeth."**

Here we learn that Zakariya, just like Abraham (pbut) before him, prayed to God for a righteous child. And like Abraham and his wife, Zakariya (pbut) was of advanced age and his wife was barren. In Islam, it is prophets whom God communicates to through angels, generally the angel Jibril or Gabriel (pbuh). Notice that Zakariya's (pbuh) prayer is answered by two or more angels. They assure Zakariya (pbuh) that ALLAH can overcome any obstacle by his act of will. Zakariya (pbuh) was granted a noble and chaste son, named Yahya (pbuh), who will also be a prophet of God. In another chapter of the Qur'an more details are presented.

Al-Qur'an 19:2
(This is) a recital of the Mercy of thy Lord to His servant Zakariya.
Al-Qur'an 19:3
Behold! he cried to his Lord in secret,
Al-Qur'an 19:4
Praying: "O my Lord! infirm indeed are my bones, and the hair of my head doth glisten with grey: but never am I unblest, O my Lord, in my prayer to Thee!
Al-Qur'an 19:5
"Now I fear (what) my relatives (and colleagues) (will do) after me: but my wife is barren: so give me an heir as from Thyself,-
Al-Qur'an 19:6
"(One that) will (truly) represent me, and represent the posterity of Jacob; and make him, O my Lord! one with whom Thou art well-pleased!"
Al-Qur'an 19:7
(His prayer was answered): "O Zakariya! We give thee good news of a son: His name shall be Yahya: on none by that name have We conferred distinction before."
Al-Qur'an 19:8
He said: "O my Lord! How shall I have a son, when my wife is barren and I have grown quite decrepit from old age?"

Al-Qur'an 19:9
He said: "So (it will be) thy Lord saith, 'that is easy for Me: I did indeed create thee before, when thou hadst been nothing!'"

Zakariya (pbuh) is worried that his family or his people will not remain righteous after he leaves this earth, so he asked God for a child that will lead them in the straight path. Zakariya invokes the memory of another righteous prophet and the father of the Israelites, Jacob (pbut). We also find that God named Zakariya's son Yahya (pbut) and this is a name that God has never given to anyone else. ALLAH then affirms the ease at which he creates everything. He reminds Zakariya (pbuh) that he and all of mankind were at one time non-existent and he made them from nothing. How much easier is it to create a child from two improbable parents?

Al-Qur'an 21:89
And (remember) Zakariya, when he cried to his Lord: "O my Lord! leave me not without offspring, though thou art the best of inheritors."
Al-Qur'an 21:90
So We listened to him: and We granted him Yahya: We cured his wife's (Barrenness) for him. These (three) were ever quick in emulation in good works; they used to call on Us with love and reverence, and humble themselves before Us.

In chapter 21 of the Qur'an, we find that God cured Zakariya's (pbuh) wife of barrenness. ALLAH informs us of the great works and character of all three members of this God-fearing family. Now we draw our attention to Yahya (pbuh).

John the Baptist (pbuh)

Al-Qur'an 19:7
(His prayer was answered): "O Zakariya! We give thee good news of a son: His name shall be Yahya: on none by that name have We conferred distinction before."

Yahya (pbuh) is considered to be synonymous with the Biblical figure John the Baptist. As mentioned above, God gave him a distinctive name. Many have assumed that Yahya and the Hebrew word for John are equivalent. With this thought in mind, they contend that the Qur'an' has mistakenly assumed that Zakariya's son was the first person named John, when the Old Testament has no less than 27 mentions of the name John.

"The fact is that the Arabic equivalent of John of the New Testament is Yuhanna not Yahya. And similarly, the Arabic equivalent of John of the Hebrew Bible (the Old Testament) is Yuhanan not Yahya. Anyone who possesses a basic knowledge of Semitic languages will straight away point out that the names Yahya and John (Yuhanan or Yuhanna) are two entirely different names. One does (sp) not need to be an expert in Semitic languages to verify this claim; a simple Arabic translation of the Bible will suffice."

http://www.islamicawareness.org/Quran/Contrad/External/yahya.html#2

For the purpose of convenience, I use the moniker, John the Baptist (pbuh). At any rate, we are told of the character and mission of Yahya (pbuh), known to many as John the Baptist.

Al-Qur'an 3:39
While he was standing in prayer in the chamber, the angels called unto him: "Allah doth give thee glad tidings of Yahya, witnessing the truth of a Word from Allah, and (be besides) noble, chaste, and a prophet,- of the (goodly) company of the righteous."

Al-Qur'an 19:12
(To his son came the command): "O Yahya! take hold of the Book with might": and We gave him Wisdom even as a youth,
Al-Qur'an 19:13
And piety (for all creatures) as from Us, and purity: He was devout,
Al-Qur'an 19:14
And kind to his parents, and he was not overbearing or rebellious.
Al-Qur'an 19:15
So Peace on him the day he was born, the day that he dies, and the day that he will be raised up to life (again)!

Al-Qur'an 6:85
And Zakariya and John, and Jesus and Elias: all in the ranks of the righteous

God describes Yahya (pbuh) as noble, chaste, a prophet, of the company of the righteous, wise even as a youth, pious, devout and kind to his parents. The Qur'an makes no mention of him baptizing people in water, but it does maintain that Yahya (pbuh) is the forerunner to a Word from ALLAH. We will soon find out who was this Word of God. From the story of Zakariya and Yahya (pbut), our attention is drawn to their close relatives from the family of Imran.

Al-Qur'an 3:33
Allah did choose Adam and Noah, the family of Abraham, and the family of 'Imran above all people,-
Al-Qur'an 3:34
Offspring, one of the other: And Allah heareth and knoweth all things.

We see here that that the family of Imran, like the family of Abraham (pbuh), has been chosen by God for a specific mission.

Mary the Mother of Jesus (pbuh)

Al-Qur'an 3:35
Behold! a woman of 'Imran said: "O my Lord! I do dedicate unto Thee what is in my womb for Thy special service: So accept this of me: For Thou hearest and knowest all things."

Al-Qur'an 3:36
When she was delivered, she said: "O my Lord! Behold! I am delivered of a female child!"- and Allah knew best what she brought forth- "And no wise is the male Like the female. I have named her Mary, and I commend her and her offspring to Thy protection from the Evil One, the Rejected."

Al-Qur'an 3:37
Right graciously did her Lord accept her: He made her grow in purity and beauty: To the care of Zakariya was she assigned. Every time that he entered (Her) chamber to see her, He found her supplied with sustenance. He said: "O Mary! Whence (comes) this to you?" She said: "From Allah: for Allah Provides sustenance to whom He pleases without measure."

This is the description of the birth of Mary, the mother of Jesus (pbuh). Mary's mother, a woman from Imran, wished to dedicate her child to the service of God. Apparently she had wished for a male child, but she conceived a female child. Still God "graciously accepted her," giving Mary and her offspring his protection. Notice that God was caring for Mary even as a child. There is an indication here that God supplied food for her specifically. So she was always blessed with God's favor. Perhaps it is because of her subsequent role.

Al-Qur'an 3:42
Behold! the angels said: "O Mary! Allah hath chosen thee and purified thee- chosen thee above the women of all nations.
Al-Qur'an 3:43
"O Mary! worship Thy Lord devoutly: Prostrate thyself, and bow down (in prayer) with those who bow down."
Al-Qur'an 3:44
This is part of the tidings of the things unseen, which We reveal unto thee (O Messenger!) by inspiration: Thou wast not with them when they cast lots with arrows, as to which of them should be charged with the care of Mary: Nor wast thou with them when they disputed (the point).
Al-Qur'an 3:45
Behold! the angels said: "O Mary! Allah giveth thee glad tidings of a Word from Him: his name will be Christ Jesus, the son of Mary, held in honour in this world and the Hereafter and of (the company of) those nearest to Allah;
Al-Qur'an 3:46
"He shall speak to the people in childhood and in maturity. And he shall be (of the company) of the righteous."

Al-Qur'an 3:47
She said: "O my Lord! How shall I have a son when no man hath touched me?" He said: "Even so: Allah createth what He willeth: When He hath decreed a plan, He but saith to it, 'Be,' and it is!

The Qur'an goes right into the discussion between Mary and the angels. It cannot be emphasized enough that ALLAH has chosen this Jewish woman, above all other women for a special purpose. Prophet Muhammad (pbuh) is articulating, to fellow Arabs at the time, that God has chosen a Jewish woman. He didn't say his mother, his sister, his wife or his daughter was chosen by God, but a Jewess. It is only natural to exalt yourself and your loved ones, yet he has exalted Mary to this esteemed position, because his words are not his own. They are direct revelation from God. In fact, verse 44 is ALLAH talking to Muhammad (pbuh), through Muhammad's (pbuh) own lips. This verse stresses that the knowledge of these events were unknown to Muhammad (pbuh). He was not there when lots were cast to determine who would be the caretaker for Mary and Zakariya (pbuh) came out victorious amidst some controversy over the outcome. Thus Muhammad (pbuh) is being informed the same time that his audience is. Then the narrative continues.

Mary is informed of this special gift from God. Though Mary's parents wanted a son to dedicate for God's service, this wish was granted to Mary. She was giving the good news of a son, Jesus (pbuh), who will deliver God' message as a child and throughout his life. The Qur'an labels Jesus (pbuh) as a "word" from God. Jesus is the "Word" from God that Yahya (pbuh) is predecessor to.

The Bible says in numerous places that Jesus (pbuh) is sitting on the right hand of God. The Qur'an clarifies that this position is not geographical, but metaphoric. And Jesus (pbuh) will not be alone. The Qur'an states that he will be in good company with the most righteous of people.

Just as the story is told in the Gospel of Luke, Mary is reluctant to believe that such a thing is possible, considering that she is a virgin. She is told that this is a small matter for God. He merely wills his decrees into existence. But this is not the end of Mary's encounters with angels.

Al-Qur'an 19:16
Relate in the Book (the story of) Mary, when she withdrew from her family to a place in the East.
Al-Qur'an 19:17
She placed a screen (to screen herself) from them; then We sent her our angel, and he appeared before her as a man in all respects.
Al-Qur'an 19:18
She said: "I seek refuge from thee to (Allah) Most Gracious: (come not near) if thou dost fear Allah."
Al-Qur'an 19:19
He said: "Nay, I am only a messenger from thy Lord, (to announce) to thee the gift of a holy son.
Al-Qur'an 19:20
She said: "How shall I have a son, seeing that no man has touched me, and I am not unchaste?"
Al-Qur'an 19:21
He said: "So (it will be): Thy Lord saith, 'that is easy for Me: and (We wish) to appoint him as a Sign unto men and a Mercy from Us': It is a matter (so) decreed."
Al-Qur'an 19:22
So she conceived him, and she retired with him to a remote place.

In this instance, Mary is confronted by one angel, in complete resemblance of a man. Mary is at first fearful of the angel, but he puts her at ease and again delivers the news of a son. Mary gives the same retort, "How can I have a son when no man has touched me" and she testifies to her own chastity. God says "it is easy for me!" She became pregnant by God's will without any male participation.

Al-Qur'an 19:23
And the pains of childbirth drove her to the trunk of a palm-tree: She cried (in her anguish): "Ah! would that I had died before this! would that I had been a thing forgotten and out of sight!"
Al-Qur'an 19:24
But (a voice) cried to her from beneath the (palm-tree): "Grieve not! for thy Lord hath provided a rivulet beneath thee;
Al-Qur'an 19:25
"And shake towards thyself the trunk of the palm-tree: It will let fall fresh ripe dates upon thee.
Al-Qur'an 19:26
"So eat and drink and cool (thine) eye. And if thou dost see any man, say, 'I have vowed a fast to (Allah) Most Gracious, and this day will I enter into not talk with any human being'"

Mary endured great pain to deliver her miraculous son into this world. And God delivered her words of encouragement and fruit to soothe and strengthen her. Mary took a vow of silence while God fulfilled his promise to her.

The words God uses to describe Mary should not be overlooked. ALLAH says that he made her grow in purity and beauty (3:37). He describes her as chaste (21:91) and devout (66:12). And most importantly, she is described as a sign and an example (21:91,

23:50, 66:11-12). Mary was a God-fearing woman. When confronted by the angel, she seeks refuge from God. The Qur'an aligns her with the wife of the Pharaoh in Moses' (pbuh) time. Both women stood firmly on the side of God in the midst of utter disbelief. The Qur'an says of Mary, "she testified to the truth of the words of her Lord and of His Revelations" (66:12).

Young Jesus (pbuh)

The Qur'an says that Jesus (pbuh) is a word of God. In Christianity, Jesus (pbuh) is called the word of God, as well (John 1:14). John's gospel tells us that the word of God created all things. Therefore Christians maintain that Jesus (pbuh) created all things. It is the Muslim view that John and Christianity as a whole have a grave misunderstanding here. The Qur'an says that Jesus (pbuh) is "A" word of God (3:45) and that word was "BE" (3:47). This is an extremely important distinction between Islam and Christianity and the Qur'an and the Bible. In the Qur'an, God creates everything by his will. He simply wills things into being. From a humanistic standpoint, he says "Be," not literally but as he wills, his will came into existence. So when he decided to make the universe, he said "Be," when he wanted to make the moon, he said "Be" and on and on. When he decided to make Jesus (pbuh) without a father, he said "Be." And the Qur'an sharply corrects any proclivity one may have to ascribe divinity to Jesus (pbuh) for his miraculous birth.

Al-Qur'an 3:59
The similitude of Jesus before Allah is as that of Adam; He created him from dust, then said to him: "Be." And he was.

If one is to place divinity upon Jesus' shoulders for being born with no father, he must also place divinity upon the shoulders of Adam (pbut) because he had no mother or father. ALLAH has created everything by his word and Jesus and Adam (pbut) are two of his words. We all are the words of God. In John's gospel, it says that the word became flesh (John 1:14), but actually all of God's words became flesh that he decreed to be human or animals. And all of his words became the material world around us. Therefore Jesus (pbuh) is not special for this title. The Qur'an is drawing attention to the greatness of God, that his decree is not limited. His word will come to fruition despite man's perception of its difficulty. Now we return to the birth of Jesus (pbuh).

Al-Qur'an 23:50
We gave them both shelter on high ground, affording rest and security and furnished with springs.

God provided Mary and her babe a safe heathen. Soon she and her son are strong enough to meet their community.

Al-Qur'an 4:156
That they rejected Faith; that they uttered against Mary a grave false charge

Al-Qur'an 19:27
At length she brought the (babe) to her people, carrying him (in her arms). They said: "O Mary! truly an amazing thing hast thou brought!
Al-Qur'an 19:28
"O sister of Aaron! Thy father was not a man of evil, nor thy mother a woman unchaste!"

Her people are perplexed by this unmarried woman and her newborn son. They allege that she has had sex before marriage. The Qur'an calls this a "grave false charge (4:156)."

It is noteworthy that the Biblical character Joseph, who is supposed to have betrothed Mary, is completely unaccounted for in the Qur'an. But according to the Bible, she was engaged to Joseph and he believed as this crowd did, that she was unchaste until he was informed otherwise (Matt. 1:19). This crime was punishable by death according to the Jewish Torah, but the Bible never explains why she was not held accountable for this capital crime. The reason might have to do with Jesus' first miracle in the Qur'an [his first miracle in the Bible is turning water into wine (John2:1-11)].

Imagine the scene: Mary's people are accusing her of having sex before marriage. What does she do? What can she do? Will she tell them that an angel came to her and that she had a child without any male involvement? Would they believe that?

Al-Qur'an 19:29
But she pointed to the babe. They said: "How can we talk to one who is a child in the cradle?"
Al-Qur'an 19:30
He said: "I am indeed a servant of Allah: He hath given me revelation and made me a prophet;

Al-Qur'an 19:31
"And He hath made me blessed wheresoever I be, and hath enjoined on me Prayer and Charity as long as I live;
Al-Qur'an 19:32
"(He) hath made me kind to my mother, and not overbearing or miserable;
Al-Qur'an 19:33
"So peace is on me the day I was born, the day that I die, and the day that I shall be raised up to life (again)"!
Al-Qur'an 19:34
Such (was) Jesus the son of Mary: (it is) a statement of truth, about which they (vainly) dispute.

In the Bible, Mary is the one who invokes Jesus (pbuh) to perform his first miracle of turning water into wine (It is untenable in the Muslim's view for a prophet of God to drank intoxicants, let alone supply intoxicants to others). In the Qur'an, Mary is attuned to Jesus' miraculous abilities, so she invokes him to defend her honor.

The Bible is silent on how Mary cleared her name and avoided punishment, but the Qur'an as a correction and completion of previous scriptures explains this for us. To this very day, there are still people who spew slanderous claims against Mary and Jesus (pbuh). Some Jews today believe that Mary was unchaste. They would rather believe that their Jewish sister was unchaste, than to believe in a miracle, when the Old Testament is filled with miracles, particularly of children being born against tremendous odds.

At that time, scribes and Pharisees were the intellectuals of the Jewish people. They knew the Jewish Torah, thus Jesus (pbuh) was a performer of miracles to convince them of his validity. Yet many still rejected him. (Not unlike the intellectuals of today, they want to be shown a miracle and we present them with the

Qur'an. And many still reject it.) Their first encounter with Jesus (pbuh) was a miraculous one.

Because of Mary's great character and bravery, ALLAH made it a point to eradicate her from the "grave false charge" made against her today (4:156), as Jesus (pbuh) did 2000 years ago. We should turn our attention to the verse in which Jesus (pbuh) says that he was "kind" to his mother and not "overbearing or miserable." Many Muslims suggest that this is directly related to Jesus' (pbuh) depiction in the story of his first miracle in the Bible, where he shows disrespect to his mother. He is said to have called her "woman" instead of "mother" and brazenly said to her "woman, what do you want with me?" The Qur'an makes it a point to clarify the character of its prophet, implying that the Gospel of John's depiction of Jesus' (pbuh) ill treatment of his mother is inaccurate.

These verses above are where the picture of the mighty prophet of Islam, Jesus (pbuh), is being painted. He is obviously a worker of miracles, yet he immediately states that he is God's servant, not God himself. Jesus' (pbuh) power and revelation are "given" to him. They are not his property. We find confirmation in the Bible that all of his power was given to him by God (Matt. 28:18). And he is to perform all the duties of a righteous man, including charity, fasting and prayer.

Of course, the gospels of the Bible can attest to the fact that Jesus (pbuh) prayed. But how did he pray and who did he pray to? Though it is largely missed, the Bible answers these questions, as well. In Matthew's gospel, we are informed that Jesus (pbuh) prayed with his face on the ground and that he was praying to God (Matt. 26:39, 27:46). Of course, the Bible says that Moses, Aaron, Abraham, and even the angels worshipped God in the same manner (Numbers 20:6, Genesis 17:3, Revelations 7:11). And we have just read that Mary prostrated and "bowed down" in worship to God (3:43). So when you see a Muslim bowing in worship to God, you must realize that he is following the example of the greatest men and women of God and the examples of angels.

The Gospel according to Jesus' (pbuh)

Jesus (pbuh) also says that God has given him revelation. Revelation is scripture that God has given to a prophet. So what is the revelation that Jesus (pbuh) was referring to.

Al-Qur'an 3:48
"And Allah will teach him the Book and Wisdom, the Law and the Gospel

Al-Qur'an 5:46
And in their footsteps We sent Jesus the son of Mary, confirming the Law that had come before him: We sent him the Gospel: therein was guidance and light, and confirmation of the Law that had come before him: a guidance and an admonition to those who fear Allah.

God taught Jesus the laws of Moses, and Jesus (pbut) was given the Gospel or Injil (Arabic). The gospel of Jesus was a confirmation and continuation of Moses' (pbut) laws for the children of Israel. But this Gospel is not to be confused with the gospels according to Matthew, Mark, Luke or John in the Bible. The Qur'an is referring to the gospel according to Jesus (pbuh). It is the words that he actually spoke, not what others wrote about him. In fact, the gospels of the Bible mention that Jesus went from town to town preaching the gospel (Matt 4:23, 9:35 Mark 1:14), but he was not preaching Matthew, Mark, Luke or John. Those are his biographies written well after Jesus (pbuh) left this earth. The Injil of Jesus (pbuh) is the words given to him by God to preach to his people. They are Jesus' (pbuh) direct quotes only. We don't give authority to the gospel of Matthew, Mark, Luke or John, but to the Gospel of Jesus (pbuh), which has yet to be found, if ever.

If we look closely, we notice that ALLAH is making a subtle point when discussing Jesus (pbuh) in the Qur'an. His name is accompanied by the phrase "son of Mary." There is great significance in this title. First, it is a testament to the great character of Mary. It is customary in many cultures to call people by the names of their parents or children as a badge of honor. For example, Abu Bakr is not this Muslim leader's birth name. But Abu Bakr means father of Bakr. His actual name is Abdullah. He is also known as Abdullah ibn Abi Qahafa, which means Abdullah the son of Abi Qahafa. Prophet Muhammad's (pbuh) father was also named Abdullah, so he is sometimes referred to as Ibn (son of) Abdullah. This is a method of honoring ones lineage, parents or children. It is also a measuring stick that one must live up to. This person would not want to bring disgrace to the family name. Remember when Mary came to her people with Jesus (pbuh), what did they call her?

Al-Qur'an 19:28
"O sister of Aaron! Thy father was not a man of evil, nor thy mother a woman unchaste!"

They are suggesting that Mary has dishonored her parents as well as her lineage from Aaron (pbuh). So when the Qur'an calls Jesus (pbuh) the "son of Mary," it is reminding us that he has brought honor to his mother and that she is one to be used as a measuring rod.

Incidentally, the Bible has traces of a similar tradition. Some people who are unaware of this tradition have mistakenly charged the Qur'an with saying that Mary was Aaron's (pbuh) actual sister. They contend that the author of the Qur'an mistook Mary the mother of Jesus (pbuh) with the Miriam of the Jewish Torah. If they had read the Bible more carefully, they would notice that Elizabeth, Mary's cousin, is called Aaron's (pbuh) daughter (Luke 1:5). She is not his actual daughter, but his descent. Jesus (pbuh) is called the son of Adam (pbuh), the son of David (pbuh) and the son of Abraham (pbuh) (Matt. 1:1). Of course, this is not to be taken literally, but to point to Jesus' (pbuh) lineage, just as the title "sister of Aaron (pbuh)" is to be taken.

The other point emphasized with "son of Mary" is the counter to the idea that Jesus (pbuh) was the son of God. The Qur'an is emphasizing the humanity of Jesus (pbuh). The belief that Jesus (pbuh) is God's son is an issue which will be addressed later in this booklet.

The Holy Spirit

Another issue addressed in the Qur'an is the identity and role of the Holy Spirit.

Al-Qur'an 2:87
We gave Moses the Book and followed him up with a succession of messengers; We gave Jesus the son of Mary Clear (Signs) and strengthened him with the holy spirit. Is it that whenever there comes to you a messenger with what ye yourselves desire not, ye are puffed up with pride?- Some ye called impostors, and others ye slay!

Al-Qur'an 2:253
Of those messengers, some of whom We have caused to excel others, and of whom there are some unto whom Allah spake, while some of them He exalted (above others) in degree; and We gave Jesus, son of Mary, clear proofs (of Allah's Sovereignty) and We supported him with the holy Spirit.

The Holy Spirit is an angel of God which carries out God's commands. In Islam, an angel is considered to be a spirit. But contrary to the Christian idea, angels cannot disobey God. Their nature is only to obey God's command. Since angels are by nature obedient to God, they all are Holy spirits. Yet the Qur'an does use the title for one angel in particular. The Angel Gabriel's (pbuh) is used interchangeably with the title "Holy spirit" in the Qur'an. This is not to say that the other angels are not Holy Spirit. ALLAH bestowed titles upon angels and prophets which fit others to differentiate the individuals in discussion.

Al-Qur'an 2:97
Say, "Anyone who opposes Gabriel should know that he has brought down this (Quran) into your heart, in accordance with GOD's will, confirming previous scriptures, and providing guidance and good news for the believers."

Al-Qur'an 16:102
Say, "The Holy Spirit has brought it (Quran) down from your Lord, truthfully, to assure those who believe, and to provide a beacon and good news for the submitters."

Al-Qur'an 26:192
This (Quran) is a revelation from the Lord of the universe.
Al-Qur'an 26:193
The Honest Spirit (Gabriel) came down with it.

We see in these verses that Gabriel (pbuh) is called the holy and the honest spirit in the Qur'an. God takes great effort to help the reader to understand that the Holy spirit is not God. In each instance, God is the authority by which this revelation is revealed and he gives the Holy spirit power of attorney, so to speak, to deliver his message. This point is further illustrated when this "Spirit" brings glad tidings to Mary about the birth of Jesus (pbuh). Mary is understandably apprehensive about the situation and the presence of the "Spirit," with its resemblance to a man. The spirit says to Mary:

Al-Qur'an 19:19
Nay, I am only a messenger from thy Lord, (to announce) to thee the gift of a righteous son.

There have been certain Christian missionaries and apologists who attempt to persuade their audience to believe that the Holy spirit in the Islam is like that of the Holy Spirit in Christianity. The more accurate statement is that the Holy spirit in Islam is similar to the Holy Spirit of the Bible, perhaps with a few exceptions, but far from the idea held by most Christians. It is obvious that the Islamic depiction of the Holy spirit is not God, but he is God's. The Holy spirit is an angel which gives glad tidings, revelation, inspiration and strength by God's command.

Jesus (pbuh) the Miracle Worker

Al-Qur'an 5:110
Then will Allah say: "O Jesus the son of Mary! Recount My favour to thee and to thy mother. Behold! I strengthened thee with the holy spirit, so that thou didst speak to the people in childhood and in maturity. Behold! I taught thee the Book and Wisdom, the Law and the Gospel and behold! thou makest out of clay, as it were, the figure of a bird, by My leave, and thou breathest into it and it becometh a bird by My leave, and thou healest those born blind, and the lepers, by My leave. And behold! thou bringest forth the dead by My leave. And behold! I did restrain the Children of Israel from (violence to) thee when thou didst show them the clear Signs, and the unbelievers among them said: 'This is nothing but evident magic.'

Like Prophet Muhammad and all the prophets of God, Jesus was given revelation by the Holy spirit Gabriel (pbut). As a baby, Jesus (pbuh) spoke the words of God to man and as this verse attests, he did so throughout his childhood and into his adult life. In the Bible, Jesus (pbuh) is said to have been in the temple speaking to the teachers as a 12 year old (Luke 2:42-47). He was listening and asking them questions. Those around him were astonished by "his understanding" and "his answers." There is a subtle point that could be missed here. The Bible says that Jesus (pbuh) asked the teachers questions, yet the people were amazed by his answers, which probably means that he was correcting the teachers as he did so often as an adult. His people often wondered how Jesus (pbuh) was so knowledgeable about scripture. The Jews asked Jesus (pbuh) how he could have such learning when he never studied. Jesus (pbuh) replied "My teaching is not my own. It comes from Him who sent me (John 7:16). In another place, he says "These words you hear are not my own; they belong to the Father who sent me (John 14:24)." The Qur'an confirms that God taught him this knowledge and wisdom.

Bart Ehrman, in his book "Jesus,Interrupted," says that there were "traditions of Jesus' miracles in multiple independent sources." The Qur'an also mentions the many miracles of Jesus (pbuh). He gave life to a clay figure of a bird, and healed the sick and blind. Jesus also resuscitated presumed dead people back to life. And he did all these miracles, "by (God's) leave." This emphasis is purposely done to demonstrate that it is God who deserves the credit for these miracles, not Jesus (pbuh). In the Bible, Jesus (pbuh) earnestly asks God to help him bring a man named Lazarus back to life. And he thanks God for his help audibly for the audience around him to hear, so that they will know that he was sent by God (John 11:1-43). The point is that God is responsible for the miracles done through Jesus (pbuh). Let us consider, Mary. She had a child as a virgin. That was a miracle, but God is responsible for that miracle, not Mary. In like manner, Jesus (pbuh) had no power to perform miracles in himself. God performed miracles through him, which is clearly indicated in the Bible (Acts 2:22)

These miracles were a testament to Jesus' (pbuh) prophethood. Many accepted Jesus (pbuh) as a prophet of God and others did not (61:14). They accused Jesus (pbuh) of witchcraft and magic. They even sought to kill him, but ALLAH was his protector and if ALLAH protects you, nothing can harm you. The Bible records several occasions where Jesus (pbuh) escaped death (Luke 4:29-30, John 10:39, Matt 12:14-16, John 7:1, John 8:59).

Al-Qur'an 3:52
When Jesus found Unbelief on their (The Children of Israel) part He said: "Who will be My helpers to (the work of) Allah?" Said the disciples: "We are Allah's helpers: We believe in Allah, and do thou bear witness that we are Muslims.
Al-Qur'an 3:53
"Our Lord! we believe in what Thou hast revealed, and we follow the Messenger; then write us down among those who bear witness."

The Qur'an affirms that Jesus' (pbuh) closest followers were the disciples. They were Muslims (those who submit to God's will) and they were called Helpers of ALLAH. In the gospel of Matthew, the disciples are said to have heard the voice of God and they immediately "fell on their faces" (Matt 17:6). This is the exact manner in which Muslims worship God, 5 times a day. Yet they, like many others, requested that Jesus (pbuh) perform a miracle to authenticate his claims of prophethood.

Al-Qur'an 5:111
"And behold! I inspired the disciples to have faith in Me and Mine Messenger: they said, 'We have faith, and do thou bear witness that we bow to Allah as Muslims.'"
Al-Qur'an 5:112
Behold! the disciples, said: "O Jesus the son of Mary! can thy Lord send down to us a table set (with viands) from heaven?" Said Jesus: "Fear Allah, if ye have faith."
Al-Qur'an 5:113

They said: "We only wish to eat thereof and satisfy our hearts, and to know that thou hast indeed told us the truth; and that we ourselves may be witnesses to the miracle."
Al-Qur'an 5:114
Said Jesus the son of Mary: "O Allah our Lord! Send us from heaven a table set (with viands), that there may be for us - for the first and the last of us - a solemn festival and a sign from thee; and provide for our sustenance, for thou art the best Sustainer (of our needs)."
Al-Qur'an 5:115
Allah said: "I will send it down unto you: But if any of you after that resisteth faith, I will punish him with a penalty such as I have not inflicted on any one among all the peoples."

ALLAH obliged their request. He also mentioned their penalty if they are disbelievers after the truth is greatly manifested to them. This seems to be a warning to those who have faith and require something miraculous after acknowledging the truth. This is because they first confessed their faith and in the next breath, showed doubt. It is they who asked of a miracle from Jesus (pbuh) which would infer that they knew that he was capable of performing miracles in the first place. To be understood and accepted, the truth does not require a miracle. So asking for a miracle is tantamount to saying, "I want more than an explanation. I want a demonstration." For this display, ALLAH makes the penalty much stiffer, if you disbelieve thereafter. Now what was Jesus' (pbuh) message and who was his message geared towards.

Jesus (pbuh) the Messenger

Al-Qur'an 61:6
And remember, Jesus, the son of Mary, said: "O Children of Israel! I am the messenger of Allah (sent) to you.

It is the Quran's position that Jesus (pbuh) was the last messenger sent to the Children of Israel. Though many assert that he was sent to all of mankind, it is recorded in the Bible that he affirms that he was "only sent to the Lost Sheep of the House of Israel" (Matt 15:24).

Al-Qur'an 43:63
When Jesus came with Clear Signs, he said: "Now have I come to you with Wisdom, and in order to make clear to you some of the (points) on which ye dispute: therefore fear Allah and obey me.
Al-Qur'an 43:64
"For Allah, He is my Lord and your Lord: so worship ye Him: this is a Straight Way."

Like all prophets of God, Jesus (pbuh) maintained the belief in One God. He was also sent to address the disputes that arose amongst the Children of Israel.

Al-Qur'an 57:27
We sent after them Jesus the son of Mary, and bestowed on him the Gospel; and We ordained in the hearts of those who followed him Compassion and Mercy.

Gospel means good news. The good news that Jesus (pbuh) brought was that of compassion and mercy. His followers exemplified these characteristics. Of course, Jesus (pbuh) and his followers' compassion and mercy were a reflection of the Most Compassionate and the Most Merciful God. These attributes that Jesus (pbuh) taught are what made him into a legend, but many have taken the meaning out of love and compassion. Jesus (pbuh) taught that you show compassion and mercy by following the laws of God.

Al-Qur'an 3:50
"'(I have come to you), to attest the Law which was before me. And to make lawful to you part of what was (Before) forbidden to you; I have come to you with a Sign from your Lord. So fear Allah, and obey me.

Al-Qur'an 3:51
"'It is Allah Who is my Lord and your Lord; then worship Him. This is a Way that is straight.'"

Jesus (pbuh) came to fulfill the laws of God that the Children of Israel had and to make some amendments to them. ALLAH makes his laws in accordance with the time and circumstances. The Children of Israel were initially a nomadic people. As such their justice was swift and heavy-handed. Over time, they lost the spirit of the law. As they settled, their judicial process had more time for deliberation. But by this time, they were in need of reaffirmation that the Law was to provide justice. It was also to provide compassion and mercy and to take into account the circumstances surrounding the transgression. Jesus (pbuh) came to illustrate these points.

The Bible is with the Qur'an on this accord. In the Gospel of Matthew, chapter 5, Jesus (pbuh) says that he does not come to destroy the law, but to fulfill it. He commands his followers to adhere to the laws down to the smallest detail. And thereafter in this chapter and the next, Jesus (pbuh) goes on to revise several commandments of the Law. Some laws he stricken and others he loosened to address the proclivities that the Children of Israel had in executing the Laws.

And again, the Qur'an records Jesus (pbuh) making it abundantly clear that we are to worship ALLAH, who is his Lord and our Lord. This is a concerted effort to demonstrate that the idea of Jesus (pbuh) being God and being worshipped does not have warrant from the teachings of Jesus (pbuh). It is of little doubt that Jesus (pbuh) repeatedly made his position as a servant of God clear. None of his followers or his enemies took him to be God. He was but a great messenger of God to the Children of Israel.

Jesus (pbuh) the Messiah

Al-Qur'an 43:57
When (Jesus) the son of Mary is held up as an example, behold, thy people raise a clamour thereat (in ridicule)!
Al-Qur'an 43:58
And they say, "Are our gods best, or he?" This they set forth to thee, only by way of disputation: yea, they are a contentious people.
Al-Qur'an 43:59
He was no more than a servant: We granted Our favour to him, and We made him an example to the Children of Israel.

Jesus (pbuh) was to be a leader and example for the Children of Israel to follow. He provided them with the good news. He was also the one on whom they were waiting.

Al-Qur'an 3:45
Behold! the angels said: "O Mary! Allah giveth thee glad tidings of a Word from Him: his name will be Christ Jesus, the son of Mary, held in honour in this world and the Hereafter and of (the company of) those nearest to Allah

The Children of Israel had long awaited a prophet of God, who would be their deliverer from oppression. They were under the rule of the Romans at the time and they were awaiting a warrior Messiah to liberate them. The Qur'an acknowledges that Jesus (pbuh) was the Messiah of the Children of Israel. Messiah means "One appointed by God." Though all prophets are appointed by God, Jesus (pbuh) had this title, "Messiah," afforded to him for the purpose of identification. Abraham is known as the "Friend of God," Moses is the "The One to whom God speaks" and Muhammad (pbut) is "the Messenger of God." All of these monikers could be used for each of these Prophets, but they are used to distinguish one from another in discussion.

"Messiah" has been translated as "Christ," which gets its origin from the Greek word "Christos." As I have mentioned, it means "One appointed by God." Unfortunately, the title "Christ" has acquired a connotation that is unfounded. Many have mistakenly attributed divinity to the word "Christ," though there is no merit for this idea. The Children of Israel were awaiting a human being appointed by God, not God himself, to guide them in the proper direction. However, they rejected the Messiah when he came to them. And to this date, they continue their wait for a Messiah which has already come.

Al-Qur'an 5:78
Curses were pronounced on those among the Children of Israel who rejected Faith, by the tongue of David and of Jesus the son of Mary: because they disobeyed and persisted in excesses.

Many of Children of Israel outright rejected their Messiah. They ignored Jesus' (pbuh) teachings of compassion and mercy, because he was not the warrior prophet that they had expected. A point to note is that they overcame their oppression without the Messiah's help, which means that they were mistaken to assume that the Messiah was to be a warrior which liberated them from the Romans in the first place. Because of Jesus' (pbuh) following and his teachings of compassion, not war, some felt it necessary to get rid of him, as he would be a detriment to their cause.

Not Killed or Crucified

Al-Qur'an 3:54
And (the unbelievers) plotted and planned, and Allah too planned, and the best of planners is Allah.

The hierarchy of the Children of Israel sought to kill and crucify this great prophet of God. And they thought that they had killed him, but ALLAH is the Best of planners.

Al-Qur'an 4:157
That they said (in boast), "We killed Christ Jesus the son of Mary, the Messenger of Allah";- but they killed him not, nor crucified him, but so it was made to appear to them, and those who differ therein are full of doubts, with no (certain) knowledge, but only conjecture to follow, for of a

surety they killed him not:-
Al-Qur'an 4:158
Nay, Allah raised him up unto Himself; and Allah is Exalted in Power, Wise

It has been believed by Christians and non-Christians alike that Jesus (pbuh) was crucified. However, the Bible has ample evidence to suggest otherwise. Here are a few reasons why one should question the crucifixion of Jesus (pbuh):

- The Bible says none of his bones will be broken. It is impossible to be nailed to a cross with none of your bones broken.
- Jesus (pbuh) begged God for hours to be saved from the crucifixion and the Bible says a just man's prayed are always heard by God. Jesus (pbuh) himself says that God always hears him and Hebrews 5:7 says that God heard his prayers to be saved him from the crucifixion. The Biblical connation of "God hears your prayers" is that God answers your prayers. Therefore God answered Jesus' (pbuh) pleas to be saved. The alternative is that God ignored his prayers to be saved.
- Jesus (pbuh) said that it is IMPOSSIBLE for him to die outside of Jerusalem. The crucifixion is said to have taken place at Golgotha, which is OUTSIDE OF JERUSALEM.
- Jesus (pbuh), Mary Magdalene, Paul and two angels said that Jesus (pbuh) was ALIVE, not resurrected. If one is resurrected, that means that you were actually dead and you came back as a spirit. When someone is said to be ALIVE, that means that they were presumed to be dead, but they are not.
- Jesus (pbuh) said that resurrected people are spirits. Jesus' (pbuh) disciple thought that he was resurrected, but Jesus (pbuh) assures them that he was not a spirit, but his same physical self. He even ate food to demonstrate that he was not a resurrected spirit.

For a more concise explanation of these points and many more, see my book, "Jesus was not Crucified."

Al-Qur'an 3:55
Behold! Allah said: "O Jesus! I will take thee and raise thee to Myself and clear thee (of the falsehoods) of those who blaspheme

As aforementioned, in the Bible Jesus (pbuh) escaped death numerous times. Thus it should come as no surprise that he escaped death from crucifixion. ALLAH saved his prophet from this humiliating death. ALLAH made it appeared that Jesus (pbuh) was being killed; meanwhile he raised Jesus (pbuh) from this great tribulation to heaven. He also promised to clear Jesus' (pbuh) name of any blasphemy falsely attributed to him.

The Corruption of Jesus' (pbuh) Message

First, God absolved Mary from any wrong doing. Then Jesus (pbuh) is rightfully attributed the title of Messiah. The Qur'an accentuates his mission. It also tells who he who his mission was for. And finally it explains that God saved his messenger from his enemies. It is apparent that Jesus' (pbuh) message was misunderstood in his lifetime, but the Qur'an suggests that his message was distorted further after his departure.

Al-Qur'an 5:12
Allah did aforetime take a covenant from the Children of Israel, and we appointed twelve captains among them. And Allah said: "I am with you: if ye (but) establish regular prayers, practise regular charity, believe in my messengers, honour and assist them, and loan to Allah a beautiful loan, verily I will wipe out from you your evils, and admit you to gardens with rivers flowing beneath; but if any of you, after this, resisteth faith, he hath truly wandered from the path or rectitude."

Al-Qur'an 5:13
But because of their breach of their covenant, We cursed them, and made their hearts grow hard; they change the words from their (right) places and forget a good part of the message that was sent them, nor wilt thou cease to find them- barring a few - ever bent on deceits: but forgive them, and overlook (their misdeeds): for Allah loveth those who are kind.

It is the Qur'an's position that the "Torah" that the Jews have today is not the actual words of God delivered to the prophet Moses (pbuh). It is writings falsely attributed to Moses (pbuh). Though they may have been inspired by the actual Torah that God gave Moses (pbuh), it is quite clear that Moses (pbuh) is not the author of the first 5 books of the Bible. This is almost unanimously agreed upon by Bible scholars. One glaring problem with this notion is that the Jewish Torah is written in 3rd person when writing about Moses (pbuh), which indicates that he is not the author. Another problem is that the Bible and its prophet said that the Laws of Moses (pbuh), i.e. the Torah, have been corrupted. "'How can you say, 'We are wise, for we have the law of the LORD,' when actually the lying pen of the scribes has handled it falsely (Jeremiah 8:8)?" The Qur'an is merely affirming what is already in their book. (For more information see my book entitled, "The Jewish Torah is not The Word of God.")

The Qur'an initially addresses the Children of Israel and the covenant that they had with ALLAH. One of their stipulations was to "believe in my messengers, honor and assist them." The Children of Israel attempted to kill Jesus (pbuh). This was an emphatic breach of their agreement with God. Even worse, they changed the message of the Messengers of God, thus causing mass confusion. In the next verse, "Christians" are mentioned.

Al-Qur'an 5:14
From those, too, who call themselves Christians, We did take a covenant, but they forgot a good part of the message that was sent them.

It is noteworthy that the Qur'an says that Christians called themselves "Christians." It is because Jesus (pbuh) never named his followers "Christians." It is but a nickname given to them after Jesus (pbuh) came and they chose to keep it. Nonetheless, the Qur'an accuses the "Christians" of forgetting a great deal of the message that was revealed to them. Now both the Children of Israel and the Christians are spoken to.

Al-Qur'an 5:15
O people of the Book! There hath come to you our Messenger, revealing to you much that ye used to hide in the Book, and passing over much

God calls them "People of the Book" and he proposes that they have hidden parts of God's message and passed over parts of it. In Matthew's gospel, Jesus (pbuh) said "Every day I sat in the temple courts teaching," yet there is very little in the gospels about his time in Jerusalem. This is further proof that his teachings were hidden. And again the Qur'an mentions their mishandling of his message.

Al-Qur'an 3:78
There is among them a section who distort the Book with their tongues: (As they read) you would think it is a part of the Book, but it is no part of the

Book; and they say, "That is from Allah," but it is not from Allah: It is they who tell a lie against Allah, and (well) they know it!

Al-Qur'an 3:71
Ye People of the Book! Why do ye clothe Truth with falsehood, and conceal the Truth, while ye have knowledge?

The evidence for these verses is the numerous interpolations, contradictions and even falsified prophecies present in the Bible. I will provide 2 examples to solidify this point. The famous verse with the phrase "the Father, the Son and the Holy Spirit... are one" in 1John 5:7 is a well-known interpolation by Bible scholars and students. Also well known amongst Biblical scholars and avid readers is the false prophecy made by the author of the gospel of Matthew. In Matthew 2:15, it is declared that God said "Out of Egypt, I call my son" as fulfillment of a prophecy from Hosea 11:1. However, if we read Hosea 11:2, we find that the person spoken of was a worshiper of the pagan God Baal. Of course, no one is willing to postulate that Jesus (pbuh) worshiped Baal, so it is clearly a false prophecy and fulfillment. Because of these discrepancies and many others is it impossible to take the entire Bible as the complete truth. The Qur'an is merely pointing out that the message has been distorted and following a distorted message is bound to lead one astray.

Al-Qur'an 5:77
Say: "O people of the Book! exceed not in your religion the bounds (of what is proper), trespassing beyond the truth, nor follow the vain desires of people who went wrong in times gone by,- who misled many, and strayed (themselves) from the even way.

The Qur'an warns the People of the Book about stretching the truth. It also teaches that they should learn from the mistakes of those in the past to avoid similar pitfalls.

Al-Qur'an 43:65
But sects from among themselves fell into disagreement

Because they passed over things in their Book and they added and subtracted from the message of God, confusion and unrest presented themselves. By this time, division was already an issue and these sects had disputes which, no doubt, originate with the tampering of Jesus' (pbuh) message. Each sect had their own set of innovated beliefs and practices.

Al-Qur'an 57:27
But the Monasticism which they invented for themselves, We did not prescribe for them: (We commanded) only the seeking for the Good Pleasure of Allah.

In this verse, ALLAH has stated that Christians were practicing something that he had not commanded them to. When you go to extremes in your religion in either direction, too lax or too strict, it is harmful and unattractive to those who are onlookers. In this particular instance, the Christians sought to separate themselves from the society as a whole and they placed restrictions of self-denial on them which were unwarranted. ALLAH does not want his people to be without the pleasures of this world. He wants them to enjoy this life but to do so in a righteous manner. For example, in Islam it is greatly encouraged for a man to marry a woman. Monasticism might oblige one to live a life of celibacy, which is not conducive to a fruitful life and void of the joys that marriage, children and family brings. And the most pressing issue with monasticism is when one is removed from society, they are less likely to effectively propagate their belief to others. One of the best forms of propagation is to be an example. One can't be an example to the uninformed and perhaps sinful society if they are estranged from that society. Fortunately for much of Christianity, the practice of monasticism has abated, though some still practice this to this day. But matters got even worse, when they began to blaspheme God.

TRINITY

One major doctrine of Christianity which was created after Jesus (pbuh) was on earth, was the Trinity, which states that God is made up of 3 distinct beings, The Father, the Son (Jesus) and the Holy Spirit. Jesus (pbuh) never taught such a thing. The 66 books of the Protestant Bible and the 73 books of the Catholic Bible do not teach this doctrine of a 3 in 1 God. 300 years after Jesus (pbuh), there was a council meeting in Nicea, where the decision was made that there was a Trinity in the Christian Godhead. Most Christians today accept this doctrine despite there being no Biblical evidence for its validity. ALLAH has this to say about the Trinity:

Al-Qur'an 5:73
They do blaspheme who say: Allah is one of three in a Trinity: for there is no god except One Allah. If they desist not from their word (of blasphemy), verily a grievous penalty will befall the blasphemers among them.
Al-Qur'an 5:74

> Why turn they not to Allah, and seek His forgiveness? For Allah is Oft-forgiving, Most Merciful.

In the sight of God, the Trinity is nothing short of blasphemy which incurs severe punishment. God asks that Christians repent from this blasphemy and he is willing to forgive them.

Al-Qur'an 4:171
> **O People of the Book! Commit no excesses in your religion: Nor say of Allah aught but the truth. Christ Jesus the son of Mary was (no more than) a messenger of Allah, and His Word, which He bestowed on Mary, and a spirit proceeding from Him: so believe in Allah and His messengers. Say not "Trinity": desist: it will be better for you: for Allah is one Allah: Glory be to Him.**

God suggests that Christians are exceeding limits in their religion which allow for falsehoods, even about God, to flourish. Also notice that the Qur'an maintains that the Trinity is not actually monotheism. Three distinct beings which are in total agreement are still 3 distinct beings. This belief system is better described as polytheism.

Al-Qur'an 5:17
> **In blasphemy indeed are those that say that Allah is Christ the son of Mary. Say: "Who then hath the least power against Allah, if His will were to destroy Christ the son of Mary, his mother, and all**

every - one that is on the earth? For to Allah belongeth the dominion of the heavens and the earth, and all that is between. He createth what He pleaseth. For Allah hath power over all things."

Here the Qur'an draws our attention to the fact that Jesus (pbuh) was the Christ. ALLAH says HE is not the Christ, meaning that God is not the appointed. He appoints. And God makes it abundantly clear here that he has ultimate power and ultimate authority over everything and everyone on earth. Had God wished to destroy Jesus (pbuh), Jesus (pbuh) and everyone else would be helpless to stop him.

Al-Qur'an 4:172
Christ disdaineth nor to serve and worship Allah

SON OF GOD?

Though most Christians believe Jesus (pbuh) to be God, you will find some who say that Jesus (pbuh) was not God, but the son of God. In Biblical terms, "son of God" meant a righteous person, but when this title is given to Jesus (pbuh), some Christians have understood the title literally.

Al-Qur'an 9:30
The Jews call 'Uzair a son of Allah, and the Christians call Christ the son of Allah. That is a saying from their mouth; (in this) they but imitate what the unbelievers of old used to say. Allah's curse be on them: how they are deluded away from the Truth!

Al-Qur'an 9:31
They take their priests and their anchorites to be their lords in derogation of Allah, and (they take as their Lord) Christ the son of Mary; yet they were commanded to worship but One Allah: there is no god but He. Praise and glory to Him: (Far is He) from having the partners they associate (with Him).

Both the Jews and Christians assigned sons to God without authority from God. Taking the words of their leaders and priests over the words of God, they fall into the same misgivings and misunderstand of their predecessors. Notice that the Qur'an asserts vehemently that God is one. This is because of the implications of God having a son. Sons are of the same nature as their father, thus an Eternal God would father an Eternal Son. But God has no beginning. No one gave God life, but in order to be God's son, God must give him life and God must have existed before his son. In this case, the son cannot share the same nature as God. The son is not completely independent as God is and he is not infinite as God is. Therefore he cannot be, as Trinitarians claim, equal with God the Father. He is of a different nature and particularly a dependent nature, thus God the Father is superior to God the Son. At this point, it is clear that a proponent of God having a son has ventured into polytheism. Yet there are some who even go so far as to call themselves sons of God.

Al-Qur'an 5:18
(Both) the Jews and the Christians say: "We are sons of Allah, and his beloved." Say: "Why then doth He punish you for your sins? Nay, ye are but men,- of the men he hath created

Now how can God have a son? How does anyone or any animal have a child? The most popular Biblical verse says "God gave his only BEGOTTEN son (John 3:16)." Every English speaking person has heard these words, but how many people consider the meaning of these words. The word "beget" is defined as:

- (typically of a man, sometimes of a man and a woman) Bring (a child) into existence by the process of reproduction.
- to procreate as the father; sire
- Give rise to; bring about.

Synonyms for "beget" include generate, breed, procreate, engender, and father. If one were to contend that God "gave rise to" a person, no Muslim would take issue with it because God gave rise to everything and everyone. But the Bible says Jesus (pbuh) is God's ONLY begotten son, which means that "give rise to" is not the proper definition for this verse because the Bible is filled with God's sons (Gen.6:2, Ps.82:6, 2Sam.7:14, Ps.89:26-27, Ex.4:22, Jer.31:9). Yet these sons of God are metaphoric, meaning righteous servant of God. The special title "begotten" given to Jesus (pbuh) can only mean procreation and sired by the process of reproduction. The idea itself is completely distasteful. And ALLAH addresses this in the Qur'an.

Al-Qur'an 112:3
He begets not, nor is He begotten.

God says that he has not fathered anyone and no one has fathered him. He has always existed and he has not had offspring. Also with the idea of fathering a child, one major piece of the puzzle is missing.

Al-Qur'an 6:100
And they falsely attribute to Him sons and daughters without knowledge; glory be to Him, and highly exalted is He above what they ascribe (to Him).

Al-Qur'an 6:101
Wonderful Originator of the heavens and the earth! How could He have a son when He has no consort, and He (Himself) created everything, and He is the Knower of all things.

In the verses above from the Qur'an, God explains that he has no counterpart, companion or spouse. With words like "beget" and "son" and "Father," a logical inquiry about a mother should follow. How can there be a father and son without a mother? Yet God says that begetting and conception does not play a part in his creation, he simply wills his ideas into a reality.

Al-Qur'an 19:35
It is not befitting to (the majesty of) Allah that He should beget a son. Glory be to Him! when He determines a matter, He only says to it, "Be," and it is.

God does not beget children because this process of reproduction is beneath God. A father and a begotten son is an incomplete equation. Many Christians wish to avoid the inevitable conclusion of a mother in this equation but Catholics have deemed Mary, the Mother of God. The Council of Ephesus decreed in 431 that Mary was "Theokotos." It literally means "The God-bearer" or the "One who gives birth to God." Here again, a council meeting is held over 400 years after Jesus (pbuh) about the nature of God. This decision has no Biblical basis. It is solely derived from some early Christians' belief that Jesus (pbuh) was God, as such, Mary has to be the Mother of God. This guides one to the understanding of a "begotten" child. Begotten by the father and conceived by the mother. This blasphemous idea conjures up an image which is far beneath God.

Now think of the status a woman would have if God had a son with her. There is little wonder why Mary has been venerated for hundreds of years. She has become a goddess herself in the eyes of many. In fact, there were Arabs in the time of Prophet Muhammad (pbuh) who worshipped Mary as God. To them and their like, the following verses sent.

> ### *Al-Qur'an 5:75*
> **Christ the son of Mary was no more than a messenger; many were the messengers that passed away before him. His mother was a woman of truth. They had both to eat their (daily) food. See how Allah doth make His signs clear to them; yet see in what ways they are deluded away from the truth!**
> ### *Al-Qur'an 5:76*
> **Say: "Will ye worship, besides Allah, something which hath no power either to harm or benefit you? But Allah,- He it is that heareth and knoweth all things."**

Notice that the Qur'an says that his signs are clear to you. What sign? This sign is that Jesus (pbuh) and Mary ate food. But what does this mean? It means they can't be God. God is self-sustaining. He needs nothing ever. However Jesus (pbuh) and his mother (this includes any other human being or animal) needed sustenance to survive. Their existence is dependent on something, unlike God who is completely independent. Not to mention the fact that consumption requires that your body use some of the food that it takes in and it releases what is left. It is quite distasteful to suggest that God relieved himself in anyway. But this is the conundrum that arrives when God is thought to be an earthly being. Thus the Qur'an is explicit in its condemnation of a worldly god who has progeny and a god who gains nutrition from earthly food. These ideas are quite blasphemous in Islam.

In the Bible, Jesus (pbuh) calls God "Father" figuratively. In fact, he instructs all his followers to call God "Father" (Matt. 6:9-13). Jesus (pbuh) tells Mary Magdelene that his father and her father are the same being, that his God and her God are also the same being (John 20:17). Unfortunately, much of Christendom has misunderstood the title "son of God" for Jesus (pbuh) as a righteous person. As mentioned earlier, to eradicate this problem, the Qur'an cleverly uses "son of Mary." The Qur'an lists 99 names of God, but interestingly enough "Abb" or "father" is not one of those names. There seems to be a conscious decision made by God to eliminate the confusion caused by this word, because it has been taken literally by billions of Christians throughout history. Despite the innumerous amount of figurative "sons of God" in the Bible, it became imperative to avoid this problem all together. And to this day, you will be hard pressed to find any Muslim of any sought who maintains that God has a son or daughter.

Al-Qur'an 10:68
They say: "Allah hath begotten a son!" - Glory be to Him! He is self-sufficient! His are all things in the heavens and on earth! No warrant have ye for this! say ye about Allah what ye know not?
Al-Qur'an 10:69
Say: "Those who invent a lie against Allah will never prosper."
Al-Qur'an 10:70
A little enjoyment in this world!- and then, to Us will be their return, then shall We make them taste the severest penalty for their blasphemies. This world's portion (will be theirs), then unto Us is their return. Then We make them taste a dreadful doom because they used to disbelieve.

The Qur'an has very strong condemnation of belittling and blaspheming God. God warns that those responsible for this innovation with be severely punished for their part in misguiding others to blaspheme God.

Al-Qur'an 5:72
They do blaspheme who say: "Allah is Christ the son of Mary." But said Christ: "O Children of Israel! worship Allah, my Lord and your Lord." Whoever joins other gods with Allah,- Allah will forbid him the garden, and the Fire will be his abode. There will for the wrong-doers be no one to help.

During his life, the Qur'an maintains that Jesus (pbuh) never claimed to be God. He clearly differentiated himself from God. But the Qur'an goes further.

Jesus (pbuh) the Witness

Al-Qur'an 4:159
And there is none of the People of the Book but must believe in him before his death; and on the Day of Judgment he will be a witness against them

On the Day of Judgment, Jesus (pbuh) will testify against the Jews and Christians who made false accusations against him. Jesus (pbuh) will certainly be asked if he blasphemed God and told his followers to worship him.

Al-Qur'an 5:116
And behold! Allah will say: "O Jesus the son of Mary! Didst thou say unto men, worship me and my mother as gods in derogation of Allah'?" He will say: "Glory to Thee! never could I say what I had no right (to say). Had I said such a thing, thou wouldst indeed have known it. Thou knowest what is in my heart, Thou I know not what is in Thine. For Thou knowest in full all that is hidden.
Al-Qur'an 5:117

"Never said I to them aught except what Thou didst command me to say, to wit, 'worship Allah, my Lord and your Lord'; and I was a witness over them whilst I dwelt amongst them; when Thou didst take me up Thou wast the Watcher over them, and Thou art a witness to all things.
Al-Qur'an 5:118
"If Thou dost punish them, they are Thy servant: If Thou dost forgive them, Thou art the Exalted in power, the Wise."
Al-Qur'an 5:119
Allah will say: "This is a day on which the truthful will profit from their truth: theirs are gardens, with rivers flowing beneath,- their eternal Home: Allah well-pleased with them, and they with Allah: That is the great salvation, (the fulfilment of all desires).
Al-Qur'an 5:120
To Allah doth belong the dominion of the heavens and the earth, and all that is therein, and it is He Who hath power over all things.

Jesus (pbuh) will categorically deny that he instructed his followers to worship him or his mother. Thus Christians and Jews should be very careful about their assessments of Jesus (pbuh) and his teaching because he will being defending and vindicating himself from falsehoods ascribed to him. It may not be enough for Christian to say, the leaders or the several councils decided that Jesus (pbuh) was God and God's begotten son. They must rely on Jesus' (pbuh) words and he never once claimed to be God in the Bible.

Al-Qur'an 19:37
But the sects differ among themselves: and woe to the unbelievers because of the (coming) Judgment

of a Momentous Day!
Al-Qur'an 19:38
How plainly will they see and hear, the Day that they will appear before Us! but the unjust today are in error manifest!

Hope

But there is still hope. We Muslims pray that our fellow Abrahamic brothers and sisters see the light before reaching this judgment. We offer correction and not ridicule for their current beliefs. Both the Bible and the Qur'an assert that God will substitute a group of people who fail to follow God's path with another group who will succeed. In a parable attributed to Jesus (pbuh) in the Bible, he tells of tenants of God's vineyard who refused all of God's servants (messengers), so God replaces them with tenants "who would produce fruit." (Matt 21:33-46) In like manner but far less ambiguous the Qur'an echoes this sentiment.

Al-Qur'an 47:38
If ye turn back (from the Path), He will substitute in your stead another people; then they would not be like you!

God's method here assures those in the privileged positions that God's plan will prevail with or without them. If God's followers deviate from the right path, this will not impede God's plan at all.

Al-Qur'an 9:32
They desire to extinguish Allah's light with their mouths, but Allah will not allow but that His light should be perfected, even though the Unbelievers may detest (it).

With respect to Jesus (pbuh), how does God perfect his light? Just as he has done in the past and in Jesus (pbuh) parable above, God sends a messenger to convey his message and continue and complete Jesus' (pbuh) mission.

Jesus' (pbuh) Successor

Al-Qur'an 61:6
And remember, Jesus, the son of Mary, said: "O Children of Israel! I am the messenger of Allah (sent) to you, confirming the Law (which came) before me, and giving Glad Tidings of a Messenger to come after me, whose name shall be Ahmad."

God looked upon the Arab people and chose Muhammad (pbuh). "Ahmad" is another name for Muhammad (pbuh). It is like Bob is to Robert. The Qur'an says that Jesus prophesied about the coming of Prophet Muhammad (pbut). It is true that Jesus (pbuh) prophesied of a "Comforter" who will come after him who will "lead mankind in ALL truth."(John 16:13) It is apparent that his own people, the Children of Israel, sought to kill him as soon as he began to deliver his message. In a hostile environment, it is difficult to concisely explain your every position. As such, Jesus (pbuh) could only present some of the truth to his listeners. This Comforter will provide ALL of the truth. Though Christians generally believe this Comforter to be the Holy Spirit of the Trinity, Jesus (pbuh) is reported as saying that God will send "another Comforter" (John 14:16) meaning that he was the first Comforter and there was another one to come. The word "another" in its original Greek form means another of the same type or nature. Therefore, this Comforter could not be the Holy Spirit but a holy spirit of the same human nature as Jesus (pbuh). That Comforter was Prophet Muhammad (pbuh).

Al-Qur'an 5:15
O people of the Book! There hath come to you our Messenger, revealing to you much that ye used to hide in the Book, and passing over much : There hath come to you from Allah a (new) light and a perspicuous Book, -
Al-Qur'an 5:16
Wherewith Allah guideth all who seek His good pleasure to ways of peace and safety, and leadeth them out of darkness, by His will, unto the light,- guideth them to a path that is straight.

This booklet is a testament to the fact that Muhammad (pbuh) came to fully explain the mission of Jesus (pbuh). The Qur'an, as the final testament of God, is called "muhiaman" in Arabic, which means "a quality control." The Qur'an is the measuring stick by which Christians (and Muslims) can judge the validity of today's Bible.

Al-Qur'an 5:47
Let the people of the Gospel judge by what Allah hath revealed therein. If any do fail to judge by (the light of) what Allah hath revealed, they are (no better than) those who rebel.
Al-Qur'an 5:48
To thee We sent the Scripture in truth, confirming the scripture that came before it, and guarding it in safety: so judge between them by what Allah hath revealed, and follow not their vain desires, diverging from the Truth that hath come to thee.

This means that the Gospels of the Bible have mistakes and discrepancies about Jesus' (pbuh) life, as well as his end. The Qur'an conveys to its reader that Jesus' (pbuh) mission was the same mission that all messengers and prophets of God had, forsake your will and follow the will of God. In Jesus' (pbuh) time, the children of Israel's will was to regain dominion and strength and they had little regard for a man offering spiritual treasures. They felt his message and miracles would stagnant the pursuit of their goals. So they sought to silence him permanently.

In the Jewish Torah, there are methods used to determine if a man is a false prophet. If he is deemed a false prophet, he is to be put to death (Deut. 13:5, Deut. 18:20). Presumably God would protect a true prophet from death. These beliefs came into play with Jesus (pbuh) and the Jews of his day. They sought to kill him, but God saved him from this gruesome death according to the Qur'an. Jesus (pbuh) was not resurrected, but rescued by God and he did ascend to heaven according to Islam. The Qur'an also says that every soul will taste death (29:57), which means that Jesus (pbuh) must also taste death. He must return.

Al-Qur'an 43:61
And (Jesus) shall be a Sign (for the coming of) the Hour (of Judgment): therefore have no doubt about the (Hour), but follow ye Me: this is a Straight Way.

Jesus' (pbuh) return will be a sign of the Last Day or the end of the world as we know it. The Qur'an does not specify how he will return, but it is without doubt that he will be as he was when he left, a MUSLIM.

There are plenty of people who would disagree with the depiction of the life of Jesus (pbuh) presented in the Qur'an. To them the Qur'an says

Al-Qur'an 3:60
The Truth (comes) from Allah alone; so be not of those who doubt.
Al-Qur'an 3:61
If any one disputes in this matter with thee, now after (full) knowledge Hath come to thee, say: "Come! let us gather together,- our sons and your sons, our women and your women, ourselves and yourselves: Then let us earnestly pray, and invoke the curse of Allah on those who lie!"
Al-Qur'an 3:62
This is the true account: There is no god except Allah; and Allah-He is indeed the Exalted in Power, the Wise.

God wishes that Muslims know and understand the life of Jesus (pbuh) so as to defend his honor and prophethood in Islam. Here the Qur'an encourages Muslims to have a debate with those who dispute the truth presented in the Qur'an and the Qur'an offers stipulations for this debate. We are asked to gather our family, to pray together and to ask God to curse anyone who lies in this dispute. These stipulations almost guarantee a cordial and honest debate. But if these terms are not met or if the dispute becomes futile the Qur'an has the Muslim's response.

Al-Qur'an 3:63
But if they turn back, Allah hath full knowledge of those who do mischief.
Al-Qur'an 3:64
Say: "O People of the Book! come to common terms

as between us and you: That we worship none but Allah; that we associate no partners with him; that we erect not, from among ourselves, Lords and patrons other than Allah." If then they turn back, say ye: "Bear witness that we (at least) are Muslims (bowing to Allah's Will).

At a minimum, the Muslim should attempt to come to the common place of monotheism with Jews and Christians. And if even this is rejected, the Muslim's retort is but "I am a Muslim."

No Distinction

Many Muslims and non-Muslims wish to anoint one prophet of God over another for whatever reason. The Qur'an repeatedly warns against this kind of thinking.

Al-Qur'an 2:136
Say ye: "We believe in Allah, and the revelation given to us, and to Abraham, Isma'il, Isaac, Jacob, and the Tribes, and that given to Moses and Jesus, and that given to (all) prophets from their Lord: We make no difference between one and another of them: And we bow to Allah (in Islam)."

Al-Qur'an 3:84
Say: "We believe in Allah, and in what has been revealed to us and what was revealed to Abraham, Isma'il, Isaac, Jacob, and the Tribes, and in (the Books) given to Moses, Jesus, and the prophets, from their Lord: We make no distinction between one and another among them, and to Allah do we bow our will (in Islam)."

A Muslim should not be in the habit of elevating and lowering the status of God's prophets. They all taught Islam in their respective time.

Al-Qur'an 6:83
That was the reasoning about Us, which We gave to Abraham (to use) against his people: We raise whom We will, degree after degree: for thy Lord is full of wisdom and knowledge.

Al-Qur'an 6:84
We gave him Isaac and Jacob: all (three) guided: and before him, We guided Noah, and among his progeny, David, Solomon, Job, Joseph, Moses, and Aaron: thus do We reward those who do good:

Al-Qur'an 6:85
And Zakariya and John, and Jesus and Elias: all in the ranks of the righteous:

Al-Qur'an 6:86
And Isma'il and Elisha, and Jonas, and Lot: and to all We gave favour above the nations:

Al-Qur'an 6:87
(To them) and to their fathers, and progeny and brethren: We chose them, and we guided them to a straight way.

Al-Qur'an 6:88
This is the guidance of Allah: He giveth that guidance to whom He pleaseth, of His worshippers. If they were to join other gods with Him, all that they did would be vain for them.

Al-Qur'an 6:89
These were the men to whom We gave the Book, and authority, and prophethood: if these (their descendants) reject them, Behold! We shall entrust their charge to a new people who reject them not.

Al-Qur'an 6:90
Those were the (prophets) who received Allah's guidance: Copy the guidance they received; Say:

"No reward for this do I ask of you: This is no less than a message for the nations."

It is God who chooses these men as prophets. He ranks them as the most righteous of men. We are only to follow their example. And this is a crowning jewel in Islam. Because we emulate the character and actions of those whom God has shown favor, instead of merely marveling over them, we are less likely to deify them. All of us have the potential to be ranked amongst the righteous or as the Qur'an describes them, "the foremost." The greatest men in human history were prophets and men of God. The two most influential men in history up to today are Jesus and Muhammad (pbut). And fortunately for Muslims, we do not have to choose between them. Judaism is one of the oldest religions on earth. Its Prophets are mighty men of God like Abraham, Moses and David (pbut). And again Muslims do not have to choose between them. They are all our prophets. They were men who submitted their will to the will of God. They were Muslim. In the Jewish Torah, we find out how the prophets prayed.

__Genesis 24:52__ And it came to pass, that, when Abraham's servant heard their words, he bowed himself down to the earth unto HaShem.

__Genesis 17:3__ And Abraham fell on his face…

__Exodus 34:8__ And Moses made haste, and bowed his head toward the earth, and worshipped.

__Numbers 16:22__ And they (Moses and Aaron) fell upon their faces

__Numbers 20:6__ And they (Moses and Aaron) fell upon their faces

If one were to look for the form of worship which the prophets of the of Jewish Torah performed, there is no doubt that it has a glaring similitude with the form of worship which 1.8 billion Muslims perform 5 times a day. Even the preparation which Muslims perform before worshipping God is to be found in the Jewish Torah.

__Exodus 40:31-32__ that Moses and Aaron and his sons might wash their hands and their feet thereat; when they went into the tent of meeting, and when they came near unto the altar, they should wash; as HaShem commanded Moses.

If we venture deeper into the Hebrew and even the Christian Scripture, we find:

__Joshua 5:14__ And Joshua fell on his face to the earth, and did worship...

__1Kings 18:42__ And he (Elijah) cast himself down upon the earth, and put his face between his knees.

__Matthew 26:39__ And he (Jesus) went a little further, and fell on his face, and prayed...

The universal Muslim greeting to one another is As-Salamu Alaikum, meaning "Peace be unto you." The words "Sholom Aleichem" in Hebrew also means "Peace be with you." And they sound almost identical to the Arabic salutation that all Muslims use. And this greeting is found on the lips of others in the Bible.

Genesis 43:23 (Joseph's steward) But he answered: Peace be with you

Judges 6:23 And HaShem said unto him: 'Peace be unto thee

1Samuel 25:6 (David tells his messengers) ...and thus ye shall say: All hail! and peace be both unto thee

1Chronicles 12:18 (the Spirit of God to David) ...peace, peace be unto thee, and peace be to thy helpers...

And Jesus (pbuh) greeted his disciples "Peace to you!" (John 20:19, 20:21, 20:26). It has been said that when a Christian or Jew becomes a Muslims that he has become a better Christian or Jew because he or she more closely follows the examples of the Prophets (pbut) sent by God.

This is why many Muslims consider the term "Judeo-Christian," without adding Islamic, a slap in the face. If Jews and Christians can set aside their differences to acknowledge their common roots, both should extend their hands to another group which shares the same root. Our differences arise with our understanding of Jesus (pbuh), but we cannot ignore the multitude of prophets with which we share common understanding.

Jews rejected Jesus (pbuh), who actually was their Messiah. So Christianity is the actual continuation of Judaism. Christians reject Muhammad who actually was Jesus' (pbut) successor. So Islam is the continuation of Christianity. This is our understanding. The Christian understanding is that the Old

Testament was replaced with the New Testament. Muslims believe that the last Testament, the Qur'an, replaced them both.

Al-Qur'an 2:106
None of Our revelations do We abrogate or cause to be forgotten, but We substitute something better or similar: Knowest thou not that Allah Hath power over all things?

The Qur'an is the revelation which man must abide by now. It is God's last testament and covenant with man and it gives us an accurate assessment of the prophets of God, including Jesus (pbuh). He was a man of great devotion, commitment and a worker of miracles, but he was a man nonetheless.

When we realize that he was a man in the very same way that we are men, we can understand that he had exemplary character. He is not to have us in awe, but to be our inspiration. When the Bible reports that Jesus (pbuh) said "pick up your cross and follow me," he is instructing his followers to bear their burdens as he burdened his. This is truly being Christ-like, to do as he did. Some people think it impossible to be a sinless human being as Jesus (pbuh) was. It may be impossible to change your past, but you have ultimate control of your future. Just think, as you read this booklet, you were not sinning. So there is a span of time, where you demonstrate your ability to avoid sin. If you can do this for a short period, then you can also extend that period. But greater than simply avoiding sin is being righteous. Jesus (pbuh) was a righteous man, who feed the hungry, healed the sick and stood for truth in the presence of imminent danger. This should be our goal and this should be the lesson that we take from the life of Jesus (pbuh); that we can make a difference in life, if we are willing to risk everything for the betterment of society and the will of God as he did. If we do this, our abode will be in Heaven with Jesus (pbuh) and others "nearest to God."

FIVE PILLARS OF ISLAM

1. Shahadah- This is the oath that every person must say and believe in order to be a Muslim. It is as follows: I bear witness that there is no god, but ALLAH and I bear witness that Muhammad is his Messenger. This is the most important tenants of Islam. Islam is vehement in its insistence that God is one, without partners or associates and this God (in Arabic ALLAH) communicates his will to mankind through exemplary men in history. These men are Prophets and/or Messengers of God and they include Adam, Abraham, Noah, Jacob, Isaac, Ishmael, Moses, Aaron, Lot, David, Solomon and Jesus (pbut). The last of the Prophets of God is Muhammad (pbuh) and he has been given a message to convey to all of humanity. That message is the same message given by all of God's prophets, submission to the will of God. The Arabic word for submission to God's will is Islam.

2. Worship- called Salat in Arabic; it is the prayer Muslims give to God/ALLAH five times a day. It is not the traditional prayer of requests for God. It is structured for the praise and remembrance of God throughout the day.

3. Charity- called Zakat in Arabic; it is the obligation on every Muslim to give 2.5% of his wealth to the poor, the sick and for travelers in need. God gives people opportunities to help others. One of these opportunities is with one's wealth, but it also includes sharing your time and effort to help others. In fact, a smile or a kind word is an act of charity and worship in Islam.

4. Fasting-During the month of Ramadhan, all Muslims are required to restrict their consumption of food and drink from sunrise to sunset. They also abstain from sexual relations with their spouse from sunrise to sunset. This is a lesson in self-restraint and a way in which one can feel the struggle of those less-fortunate. This is also a time to reacquaint one's self with the Qur'an and to renew their commitment to following the decrees set forth in Islam.

5. Hajj- This is the largest pilgrimage in the world. It is a pilgrimage to the holy city of Mecca and it is required of all able bodied Muslims, who can afford it, at least once in their life. Every Muslim, whether rich or poor, black or white, short or tall are all brothers and sisters. We all pray in unison in one direction, at the same time and using the similar words in praise to God and this pilgrimage is the ultimate manifestation of the oneness of the 1.8 billion Muslim community.

BOOKS BY THIS AUTHOR INCLUDE:

"ISLAM IS THE TRUTH"
"JESUS WAS NOT CRUCIFIED"
"THE JEWISH TORAH IS NOT THE WORD OF GOD"
"THERE IS NO TRINITY"
"25 MYTHS ABOUT ISLAM"
"GOD THE IRRESISTIBLE"
"FAQs ABOUT ISLAM"
"WHAT GOD SAYS ABOUT JESUS"

FOR INFORMATION ON PURCHASING THESE BOOKS
LOG ON TO
WWW.ISLAMISTHETRUTH.ORG

ABOUT THE AUTHOR

Mr. Campbell was raised attending both the Christian Church and the Muslim Mosque. He was always inquisitive about religion. Around the age of 14, he decided that Islam was the path for him. However, he was rather secretive about his belief due to the negative perception many had of the religion. When Islam became the topic of any discussion, he maintained the Islamic sympathizer role as the son of a Muslim, while being careful not to be identified as a Muslim himself. The stigma surrounding Islam and Muslims only intensified throughout the years, but so too did his desire to announce to the world that ISLAM IS THE TRUTH. Throughout his life, he had engage others in discussions on religion and a little over three years ago he realized that the issues that were raised in debate and in dialogue were issues which warranted extensive details, evidence and explanations. Drawing from all the books, lectures, and debates he come in contact with, and all the talks with Muslims, Christians, Jews, Hindus, atheists and agnostics, he set out to write one book which would convince all of the truth about the God of the universe. This one book blossomed into eight books which are written with the primary goal of proving the validity of Islam. It is with his sincerest effort that he wrote these books, with the hope that all readers will set aside their preconceived ideas and have an open mind.

Made in the USA
Charleston, SC
30 November 2013